GOD'S LOVE BROKE THE CHAINS OF SHAME

CHYWANDA FAYE WATSON

ISBN 978-1-4958-1381-8
eISBN 978-1-4958-1382-5
Library of Congress Control Number: 2017904364

Scriptures are from the Holy Bible, King James Translation

Published August 2017

INFINITY PUBLISHING
1094 New DeHaven Street, Suite 100
West Conshohocken, PA 19428-2713
Toll-free (877) BUY BOOK
Local Phone (610) 941-9999
Fax (610) 941-9959
Info@buybooksontheweb.com
www.buybooksontheweb.com

DEDICATION

I dedicate this book to my LORD and SAVIOR, JESUS CHRIST who is the lover of my soul and to every child, teenager, and adult who may have experienced abuse at the hands of another; to my children whom I love dearly and to my Spiritual Parents for teaching the Word of God to me.

PURPOSE

I wrote this book because I wanted to help heal hearts. As a child, after the abuse ended, I wanted to know if there was someone who was willing to take the time and listen to what I had to say. I wanted to know if there was anyone who could relate to what I had experienced and whether or not it was possible to go on with life. To live and thrive, instead of just surviving. I needed someone to assure me that everything was going to be all right and that what happened to me was not my fault. I carried the pain and at times, the blame for what happened to me. If it wasn't my fault, why did I feel this way?

As I got older, I needed someone to teach me about relationships. Was it okay to say no when someone wanted to take the relationship to another level? Did they mean it when they said, "I love you" or was it just a way for them to get me to fornicate with them? Most would consider this action sex, but The Holy Bible refers to sex outside of marriage as fornication. I didn't understand why things happened, but I knew what I had experienced before and after the years of abuse, would be used for a purpose. I knew I would have to use my experience to help someone else. How could anyone not want to help someone avoid all of this pain when given the opportunity?

It has taken me forty-five years to release the anger, and it was only after I surrendered my life to The LORD that I began to heal. I found out HE was not responsible for my pain or for what happened to me, because *God is Love. (I John 4:16)* Love doesn't hurt. This is love: *not that we loved God, but that HE loved us and sent His Son to be the propitiation for our sins. (I John 4:10)* I also found out I could not go through life harboring unforgiveness. *Forgive and ye shall be forgiven. (Luke 6:37)* Unforgiveness will cause you to hold on to the anger when what you need to do is release it. Holding on to the anger will not stop the person or persons who hurt you from going on with their lives, so why allow it to keep you from living yours? You must forgive and THE HOLY SPIRIT, THE COMFORTER, will help you because *HIS grace is sufficient for thee: for HIS strength is made perfect in weakness. (2 Corinthians 12:9)* This means whatever you are struggling with and are finding hard to do, HE is always there to strengthen, encourage, and most of all love you. *You can do all things through CHRIST which strengthens you. (Philippians 4:13)* I want you to know that in order to heal properly and have an abundant life, you have to let it out and as you let it out, receive the love THE LORD has for you. HIS love will begin to enter your heart and make you whole from the inside out. You will be able to forgive; *yes*, forgive those who hurt you. Satan won't be able to torment you with the memories and the guilt of what happened. You won't feel inferior to others. There won't be a need to compare yourself to others because you love yourself for who you are. You will be thankful to GOD for the way HE made you. You won't seek out someone else to fill the emptiness and loneliness in your heart because the love of THE LORD is there and nothing and no one can replace His love. You will be able to avoid fornicating (sex outside of marriage) in order to keep someone in your life. You will be able to say, "I am NOT fornicating, having sex or whatever you want to call it until I get married." You won't have to hurt, degrade, or sacrifice your body anymore. You can cherish your virginity until you get married or if you are no longer a virgin, you can be celibate and wait on THE LORD to send you your husband. It is all right to say, "NO." You are the child of THE MOST HIGH GOD, THE ONLY TRUE AND LIVING GOD, THE KING OF KINGS AND THE LORD OF LORDS and don't forget it. You will be able to love others because of the love THE LORD is showering over you. HE LOVES YOU AND YOU CAN TRUST HIM.

My prayer is that you will be blessed by my testimony and THE LORD will heal you and love you during this process. GOD BLESS YOU.

TABLE OF CONTENTS

CHAPTER 1

Scripture: Proverbs 12:29-He that troubleth his own house shall inherit the wind: and the fool shall be servant to the wise of heart.

I believe satan knew something about a particular baby girl who was to be born on August 18, 1968. He knew THE LORD was going to use her, so he had to find a way to destroy her before she was born. He also knew that her father had an overwhelming appetite for sex and was willing to satisfy his appetite, regardless of what was going on with his family. The day before I was born, my mother was in the early stages of labor and when my father came home, instead of taking her to the hospital first, he had sex with her. Who does that to a woman and a child you are supposed to love? If you are familiar with the position babies are in at the time of birth, then you know the head is toward the "exit." Doctors can actually feel the baby's head when they are in that position.

While my father was having sex with my mother, my position changed. When my mother was taken to the hospital, her blood pressure was fluctuating and the doctor thought he would lose her. The doctor told my grandmother to choose. She had to make a decision about who she wanted the doctor to save — her daughter or her granddaughter. I ended up in a breech position which meant that my bottom was coming out first instead of my head and this was causing my mother's blood pressure to fluctuate. My grandmother chose her daughter because she did not know me BUT GOD KNEW ME! THE LORD, my REDEEMER, who formed me in my mother's womb, chose both of us **(Isaiah 44:24, Psalms 139:13)**. The doctor delivered me and after all of the trouble I gave my mother on the delivery table, she still loved me. She forgave my father also. She gave me a very pretty name and that was Chywanda Faye.

I grew up in a family that appeared to have it all together. My father's parents owned land and were very successful in the farming business. My father worked for my grandfather, so he had a stable income. My grandfather loved his children and he was concerned about their well-being, so if they were unemployed, it was because they chose to be that way. Like most families, arguments took place and people disagreed. I remember once my grandfather and father got into an argument about the farm and I actually witnessed a gunfight! Being four years old, this was exciting because they were actually shooting at each other! It was like an old western! My grandmother was calm and the only thing she said was, "Get away from the door" and we did. After the shooting was over, my dad had a little blood on his face from shattered glass and grandfather didn't have a scratch. My father was so angry that he gathered up his family and left. These were the "good times."

THE LORD has always been watching over us, because on that day both my grandfather and father should have been severely injured or killed. My grandfather was always the businessman. He rarely ever gave his grandchildren money without having them earn it first. We had to chop and pick cotton or pick up trash before he would give us anything, especially money. The highest amount he would pay was fifty-cent and we were excited because he would load us up on the back of the truck and take us to the store to spend our "hard earned money." He was the best! My grandfather was set in his ways, but the best thing about him was he always had money. THE LORD prospered him. He had acres and acres of land that reaped soybeans, cotton, wheat, and peach trees. I really enjoyed the peach trees. He would warn his grandchildren about eating peaches that were not ripe and if we were patient, he would harvest peaches for us when the time was right. That was good and challenging, because we could actually see the peaches on the trees. It was hard to resist the temptation of getting a closer look to determine for ourselves if the peaches were ripening according to a child's standard. To us, a small patch of red equaled ripe! We had to get a closer look so, when we wanted a treat without my grandfather's permission, we would attempt to sneak and eat the peaches that were ready to be eaten. We would walk around to each tree and knock peaches down and be finished and out of the field before my grandfather returned home. We made sure no evidence was left behind, so we thought. Being children and thinking like children, we missed a very important piece of information. When you walk on soft dirt, your footprints are there in plain sight. We were leaving evidence and didn't even know it. This is how my grandfather knew we had been eating his peaches, but we never figured it out until we got older. My grandfather was so smart!

My grandmother was a very strong willed woman. She could carry her own weight which meant she could take care of herself. She loved fishing and I would be so excited to see what kind of fish she had caught when she returned home. My grandmother caught an eel once and that was the first and only eel I have ever seen. It didn't look like a wallet at the time and I was not going to touch it to see if it was soft like the wallet either. I don't know where my grandparents got their work ethic, but you had to "earn your keep" at their house. They were not perfect, but they were all right with me. Like my grandfather, my grandmother also had rules and one rule was about the fish she would catch for the family dinner. It was simple, if you want to eat it (the fish), you had to clean it and it did not matter how old or young you were. This is when I learned how to clean fish. It was interesting to see the inside of the fish because the outside was so plain, but when you cut it open, the insides had to be pulled out and to a child, that was an amazing and exciting experience.

My maternal grandparents had a large family. My grandfather died when my mother was a teenager, so my grandmother raised her and her siblings the best way she could. Although some were grown, all total my grandmother had sixteen births with the deaths of three infants which meant there were thirteen children to raise. Going to church was very important to my mother's family. They could sing gospel songs so well, until you would literally start to cry. It was a gift from GOD that my grandparents nurtured. This was different from my father's family because everyone went to church at some point every now and then.

My mother was very pretty and still is. Her hair at the time was long, black and wavy. Her skin was very smooth and she took good care of herself. As a small child, we would go bike riding together. I would be riding my bike with training wheels and she would be patiently riding beside me. These were the "good times." I thought she was the best mother a little girl could have and I didn't want anything to come between us. She worked at one of the local factories and this allowed her to earn money and be independent. My earliest memory of my oldest brother who is three years younger than me is probably when I was five years old. He was a quiet child for the most part, but I was jealous of the attention my mother was giving him. Being a talkative five-year-old, with a mind of my own, I felt I had to say something about this situation, so I confronted my mother and told her that I felt she loved "him" more than she loved me. I didn't know his name, but I knew that he was a "him." She was shocked because I could see the expression on her face and then she pulled me close and reassured me that she loved me also. I must say I handled the situation very well considering my age. My mother was a gem! My relationship with my father was confusing to say the least. There were times when I felt he had great potential to be a wonderful father and these were the times when the family was gathered together. We would visit his parents and have cookouts. We would listen to music and everyone would sing and dance. My cousins would come over and we would have a wonderful time. It was just great, but then things began to change. I assume that it was time for me, at the age of five to become a "big girl."

CHAPTER 2

Scripture: Matthew 18:6-But whoso shall offend one of these little ones which believe in Me, it were better for him that a millstone were hanged about his neck, and that he were drowned in the depth of the sea.

I was five years old when the "lessons" began. I say this because this is the earliest memory I have. My father felt it was important for me to learn and be prepared for relationships with the opposite sex; I guess you would call them boys because I was only five. Of course at five, I did not understand what he meant or why it was necessary to learn these things. After each session of sexual abuse, he would say, "Don't tell your mother, because she will be mad at you." I didn't want that to happen because she loved me so much and so it was important to keep the secret no matter the cost. He would say, "I love you" and that confused me because he didn't see the pain he was causing. He did not see a broken spirit. He did not see me — his daughter.

The first lessons occurred between the ages of five and seven. My mother worked second shift at the factory and she would leave for work between two-thirty and three. I can remember not wanting her to go to work even begging her at times to stay home, but I couldn't tell her why. I would play with my toys hoping that something would happen to cause her to miss work. Whenever she pulled out the uniform, I would begin to feel sad and there was nothing I could do about it. I knew that as soon as she left and my father came home from work, I would be taught more "lessons." Some lessons involved fondling his private part, whether it was moving it around or pumping it. Some lessons involved him positioning his private part on me while applying pressure to my genital area. Most of the lessons took place when my brother was asleep or when he was in the living room playing with toys or watching television. After the lessons, I would have to clean myself up, and then pretend like nothing ever happened. Pretend as if it was not affecting me. This was the "norm." I had to adjust. Adjusting is something I would be doing for a long time. I had to do what was necessary to wrap my mind around what was happening. My mother rarely came home early, if anything, she would have to work a double shift. There was one occasion when I got a rash in my genital area and my mother asked me about it and as a very good secret keeper, I told her that I did not clean myself well after using the bathroom. She believed me and I stuck with that story because it worked. There were times when I wanted to tell my mother, but I would remember what my father said, "Your mother will be mad at you," so I had to go along with the program and enjoy the times the lessons did not take place. I had to adjust mentally and emotionally and at the age of five, that was difficult because I thought I was being punished for something that I did not do. If I could only ask for forgiveness so the lessons could stop. Why couldn't my father see me? Why didn't he realize what he was doing to me? He was destroying me bit by bit.

My father, in teaching me to be prepared for future relationships, failed to realize that there would be consequences. By the age of six, I had mastered what is known as masturbation. I didn't know what it was called, but I knew that there was something going on down there. One day, I was playing with my doll, and I felt it was necessary for me to get some practice in before the next lesson. I placed the doll between my legs and my mother walked in and caught me. I was not a stupid child. I knew I had to get out of the house as quick and as soon as possible. While she was looking for the belt, I ran as fast as I could out of the house. She found the belt and the chase was on. We were running lapse around the house and instead of crying like most children who are about to get a spanking would be, I was laughing. Why? I don't know why, but I think I was afraid of receiving unfair punishment. It wasn't my fault that I knew how to do this. I did not teach myself these things, but I was being punished for doing them. Eventually she caught me, but she was too tired to whip me the way she intended, and I screamed for my life. I had to play the part. After all of that, she failed to ask me the most important question and this is where parents mess up and miss the moment of truth. She didn't ask me a particular question and had she done so, as a six-year-old, processing this question with a six-year-old mind, I would have told her the truth. If she had asked, "Who taught you how to do that?" I would have opened up, and told her "who taught me."

I would have dreams that I considered nightmares. In the dreams, people would be floating around in a room that was very dark, but I could see them. They would be having sex and the force from the men would be so harsh and rough until the women would begin to bleed and there would be blood everywhere. There was so much blood coming from the women until the entire room was bloody. The women were crying and the men were laughing. There was no mercy. I would wake up afraid, but I couldn't tell anyone. I didn't have the luxury of calling momma into the room so she could hold me and tell me that it was all a bad dream. I knew I wasn't going to call my father. That would have been insane.

When I entered the first grade, things were kind of awkward. It seemed that way because I didn't attend head start very often. There had to be something I could control and going to school was just the thing. I would get up in the morning and get dressed, but not for school. I would stay in my room until the bus passed by my house and then I would walk into the living room to enjoy my day. School was boring because I would have to sit with children I didn't know and obey a woman who only wanted me to color and write letters. During snack time, I could only have a piece of a graham cracker and what I thought was a sip of juice. This was not the life I wanted as a child. It wasn't fun. I wanted excitement. I wanted to be at home with my mother. That's what I wanted and that's what I got. She was having an exciting day at home and I wanted to be a part of that excitement because there were very important things that had to be done. For example, she had clothes to wash and I had clothes to play in while they were hanging on the line. This was so much fun! The house was always clean and I was happy about that because cleaning was not for me. My mother would cook lunch for my father and we would jump into the SS Nova to take him his lunch and act like a loving family. Make believe was an adventure! This is why school was not a priority for me. I didn't even attend the graduation ceremony. My cousins told me about it, but I was not impressed. I felt this way because my mother could and would buy anything I wanted, so what they had to offer wasn't a big deal. Believe me when I say it wasn't a priority. One Christmas, the school was giving away toys and the girls could receive a black baby doll if we climbed the ladder to the second floor to receive it. It was a ladder, not stairs and I knew the difference even if I was only a child. I saw the other little girls in line and then I saw the beautiful black baby dolls. I really wanted one, but then I began to focus on the ladder and how high it was from the ground and that is when I made an important decision, NO DOLL WAS WORTH RISKING MY LIFE FOR! My aunt was trying to make me feel as if I missed out on something after we left. She was bragging about the little girls who received the doll but little did she know I was talking back to her in my mind. I was saying things like, "I don't care about a doll, because my momma will get me anything I want including a baby doll." I thought my momma could do just about anything when it came to giving me things. Now let's get back to first grade, shall we.

I didn't have friends when I was in the first grade. I just encountered the friends of my cousins, you know — classmates. The teachers were nice, but again, there were those who were not concerned about the whole child. I say this because after lunch, the students in the first grade were allowed naptime. When I should have been resting like the other children, I felt it was necessary for me to tell my teachers about my parents and what I would hear during the night. I told my teachers about what my parents were doing in the bed. Not once did they seem concerned about this first grader telling them about grown folks business. Not once did they correct the child that was standing before them, as a matter of fact, they seem intrigued as if it was juicy gossip. This is how attentive they were. Their reaction was confusing at first, because I knew that it was wrong, and I could not understand why they did not send me back to my mat or even tell my parents about what I had said. Never once did they ask me anything about me or how I understood sexual things at such a young age. If they had asked, I would have told them, because my father did not say that they would be mad at me. No one asked the right questions. I also found it interesting that on the days I tried to take a nap during naptime, they would call me up to the desk and ask me to share more information about my parent's sex life and what other things I had heard. What kind of teachers did I have?!!!

First grade was also difficult because I was still be taught the "lessons." I didn't understand why my father could not see that he was hurting me in every way imaginable. I did not want to learn this stuff! At school, it was difficult for me to play with the other children. I was withdrawing from life. I couldn't relate to the happy first grader because my childhood was slowly slipping away. My enthusiasm was weakening because I had to act as if everything was okay, everything was normal. What was normal? It was a lie. It was difficult to walk to the cafeteria and this is the place where most children love to go because there was food and the people could really cook! I remember dragging myself from one part of the school building to the other, just in a daze. I tried to be excited about what I was learning, but I was having a hard time and I couldn't tell anyone. I did find one thing at school that brought me some joy and that was reading the Dick and Jane books. Those were the best! However, if I had had the same option in first grade that I had in head start, I would have stayed home with my mother.

There were times when my parents were not able to pick me up from school and it was those times when I would go to my godparent's house. My godfather's name was Lonnie. He was the best father a girl could have even though he was not my biological father. He did not have teeth and rarely wore his dentures. He also had asthma and emphysema because he smoked cigarettes for a long time. To help him breath during the night, he would have to swallow a teaspoon full of vapor rub. I thought that was terrible, but he had to do it. My godfather was the kind of father who did not require me to give up anything to receive his love. Because he did not have teeth, he was very creative when it came to eating apples and I enjoyed every bit of it. He would cut the apple in half leaving the skin on and with a spoon, gently rake the inside of the apple and we would have apple sauce. He would feed it to me and we would enjoy apple sauce together. We didn't do a lot of things together, but I was safe with him. He didn't let anyone, if he knew about it, hurt me.

I was told stories of how independent I was even at the age of two. My godparents lived a few houses from the local high school and they would allow me to be outside to see the big kids come home from school. My godfather would get the milk crate for me and allow me to sit on it in the middle of the sidewalk, so as the kids walked by their house they would have to walk around me because that was "my sidewalk" and he dared them to touch me. My godfather was my bodyguard and he did not play about his little princess named Chywanda. I was a mischievous baby and I don't remember being that way. Really, I don't remember. I liked coffee when I was a baby and when I saw a cup, I had to have it. One time, my father had just made him a hot cup of coffee and I wanted some. Apparently, it wasn't cooling fast enough for me, so I pulled the cup and the coffee spilled on me. As they were pulling my dress off, my skin was peeling off with it. I had burns on my arm and my stomach. I also had a dog and when he would bite me, I would bite him back. I was not afraid of anything when I was a baby!

The LORD always provided a balance for me. On one side, Daddy Lonnie was busy loving and nurturing me and my biological father was busy destroying me. My godmother's name was Bessie. She was a very strong and caring woman. When I was growing up, I thought she was kind of strict, so I was very careful about what I did and the way I spoke around her. She could really cook and I just enjoyed being in her company. I could be a little girl who was pretty and strong, not afraid, ashamed and disgusting. She told me once, that she asked my mother if she could adopt me, but my mother told her no. Had the adoption taken place, my last name would have been Brown. I am very grateful that I had the opportunity to be a part of their lives because they are in Heaven now.

I don't think my parents were stable in their relationship because the communication and the understanding of what the other person said, was misunderstood. I say that because they forgot to pick me up from school one time. At the end of school one day, the students were escorted outside to meet their parents. I looked and looked and my parents were not there. I began to cry. What was I to do and then all of a sudden someone (THE HOLY SPIRIT) said gently, "Put your big girl shoes on because you will have to walk across the big highway. I took a deep breath after I stopped crying and started walking. I was still hoping that my parents would show up. I know THE LORD has always been watching over me and THE HOLY SPIRIT who is my guide, told me how to get to my godparents house. I was so afraid because there were big, mean dogs on both corners and this six-year-old did not want to go near them! I followed the crowd across the big highway and ran to my godparents house and was greeted with a "Where are your parents?" and a reply of "They did not pick me up." My godfather treated me to some apple sauce and they called my parents and can you guess what they did? Go ahead, guess? You are absolutely correct, they blamed each other! What kind of parents did I have for real?! What else could I go through? Could things get any worse?!

CHAPTER 3

Scripture: Philippians 4:7-And the peace of God, which passeth all understanding, shall keep your hearts and minds through Christ Jesus.

I don't remember seeing my mother and father argue very often, so I was shocked when my mother told us that they would be separating and that we would have to leave our home. We saw our father often and whenever he found the opportunity to "teach" me, I had to learn. It didn't matter to him. He was going to teach me whether it was in the house or in the car on the side of the road. After the separation, my mother had to find a place to live and she thought we would be able to live with my grandmother, but that didn't happen. My grandmother would only allow my mother and my baby brother to live with her so that meant my older brother and I would have to live with my father and his family. He was living with his parents at the time, but my brother and I lived down the road with my aunt and her family. My father didn't know much about taking care of children and because my aunt and her husband had children, it was only natural that we live with them. My father was so disconnected that he enrolled me in the wrong grade. I was supposed to be in the second grade and he had the school administration to place me in the fourth grade. What an experience that was! The students in the class looked much older than I did and they were clean. Clean in that their clothes looked nice. I was wearing hand-me downs and sometimes they were the right size and other times you could tell that they belonged to someone else. I didn't look like them. My hair was combed once or twice a week and my clothes were not pressed every day.

At school, there were days when I was just visible. I sat in my desk quietly so that I wouldn't draw attention to myself. I would watch the other students interact with one another as if they knew exactly what to do and the teacher would explain the activity to the groups, but I would sit in my desk quietly because I didn't know what they were talking about. The feeling of being different and knowing that I would receive an F on every assignment was crushing and I was desperate to find a way to turn things around even if it was just in the way I viewed the letter F. I was given an idea from no one other than THE HOLY SPIRIT but at the time I didn't know where the idea came from, but it worked. I began to see the F as the initial of my middle name, Faye, so when the papers would be passed out and I received mine, the F that was written in red, was for Faye instead of failure. It felt good to view it in a different way and The Lord was preserving my soul, the soul of a wounded little girl — thank you JESUS!

My aunt, like I mentioned before, lived down the street from my grandparents. My aunt was a very sweet and compassionate woman. She allowed my brother and me to live with her even though she had seven children of her own. What a woman and I must add what a man my uncle was to share his home and food with children who could eat well! She never complained about us being in her home and she never mistreated us. However, that doesn't mean we were not abused. Her husband was the type of father who said what he meant the first time. There wasn't any room for if's, and's or but's. He demanded respect from everyone who came into his home. Whenever my aunt became frustrated with the children, she would call my uncle. He would be sitting in the back area of the house in his favorite chair and he would say, "Sit down in there." By our reaction, you would have thought he was coming after us with the belt. We would be running so fast and he would be sitting in his favorite spot. He had that much power in his voice. He was truly the "man of his house." The strength in his voice was backed up by the strength of his body. My uncle never lifted weights, but he had muscles. He was a farm worker and sometimes they had to put down pipes, so his weights came in the form of manual labor. My uncle wasn't a mean man, but he raised his children to be obedient and when they were disobedient, he didn't have a problem disciplining them. One time, me and some of my other cousins were sitting in the living room and my uncle came in with one of his sons. He had been disobedient and my uncle was preparing to whip him. At first, we thought it was funny and kind of interesting that someone was going to get a whipping, but when we heard the screams, it was no longer funny and the living room was too close to where they were, so we went outside to separate ourselves from the situation just in case he remembered something we had done.

When my grandparents weren't home, my father would "teach" me. As I got older, the "lessons" became more involved. I was being positioned underneath him while he did whatever he needed to do. There were times when it felt like I would be ripped apart and the sad thing about it is I didn't know what was down there. After each session, I had to clean myself up and pretend as if nothing ever happened. Pretend that I loved my father with all of my heart. Pretend that he could do no wrong. Pretend that he was the best father — pretend, pretend, pretend! What does that do to a child? Pretending leads to manipulation and manipulation involves lying. Yes, this is another lesson that was not intentionally placed in my father's lesson plan for the day, but it is a lesson I learned. Why couldn't he just leave me alone?! Didn't he realize I was his daughter — his child? Why couldn't he see me? I needed my mother but would I tell her — probably not. I had to keep the secret.

There were times when I thought we wouldn't see our mother again. Had she forgotten us? One day at school, I was so hungry and became very weak. You have to understand that my being hungry had nothing to do with my aunt and uncle not providing us with food, but when a child is being abused in any manner, they don't have it in them at times to focus on things that should come naturally like eating. How could I focus on anything other than what my father was doing to me? It consumed me because I didn't know if I would be able to relax and be a child on that day. He would take me and my cousins riding and he would drive for so long until they would go to sleep and that's when he would reach over and start fondling me and there was nothing I could do. Again I asked, "What kind of man was this?" What kind of father was this? Why did my mother marry him? The answer to that question came later and she married him to get out of her mother's house. When women want to escape from their parent's house, my advice is to be very cautious about using marriage as an escape route because you don't know who you will end up with.

As I mentioned before, I was hungry and weak, so I left the lunch line because it was extremely long. I started walking up the hall while holding on to it with everything I had saying to myself, "Help me, would someone please help me." As I was walking, I noticed that most of the teachers were out of their rooms, but I didn't stop. I came to a classroom and I could hear someone talking and as I entered the room, I saw a woman who appeared to be an angel. She called the principal and he contacted my aunt to let her know that he would be bringing me home. My aunt worked in the cafeteria at a Catholic school and she was able to bring food home that was left over. On that day, she brought cake with apple sauce on top and just being with her made the cake taste so much better. I was so happy because I had my aunt all to myself; she was just that special to me.

Sometime after that incident, my mother came and picked us up. We landed in a town called Duncan. I went from having indoor plumbing at my aunt's house to having an outhouse and a water pump on the outside of the house. I met people who knew about me before I knew them. I was very upset. I wasn't upset with my mother for picking us up, but I was very upset with the children who supposedly got permission from my mother to say my name! What right did they have to call me Faye! I was not pleased. I didn't know these people! After about thirty minutes, I came down from my high horse due to the urging of my mother, and I gave those children a chance to know me. You have to understand it was a big adjustment for me. Before the separation, I had everything I wanted in regards to material things. I had my own room, my own toys, my own toilet that flushed, a tub with running water and all the food I could ever want. In Duncan, we had an outhouse with maggots and water that had to be pumped into a bucket. I refused to use the outhouse! No way, no how was I going to willing place my bottom above maggots and you know I found a solution to that problem (smiling). We had a field behind the house and all I needed was tissue and of course when we didn't have tissue, newspaper rubbed together was just as soft as the tissue. I had to do what I had to do. We had to take baths in a foot-tub. There was one heater in the house, so during the winter months, we would gather around it while getting dressed for school. The room we slept in had wooden floors and if you looked closely, you could see the ground. It was cold and my mother placed blankets on us to help us stay warm. GOD was working miracles because HE kept us warm to see another day. We were poor! I didn't know what was going on and why I had to suffer? I was in the middle of a whirlwind called, "**SEPARATION.**"

My experience in Duncan would be one that would have a great impact on my life. It provided time away from my father. The house we lived in belonged to my mother's boyfriend's mother. We called his mother "Mutt-Dear." Why, I don't know, but she was very kind to us. She worked for a white family in town to earn extra money and when we didn't have food, they would give us a little food to get through the day. She adored my mother and wanted her to be happy. She didn't side with her son if he was mistreating my mother. Whatever she had, she would share it with us. I was amazed at how she welcomed us into her home and helped take care of us. What kind of woman would treat people who were not even related to her so kind? She was different from my grandmothers' because she was kind to everyone.

During my stay in Duncan, I learned to appreciate the small things in life. We didn't have a television, but we had a small radio and I would listen to music and stare out of the window as a way to escape poverty. We were poor and coming from where I was before, I had to adjust to having a small amount and I learned to take care of the little that I had. I no longer had the hand-me-downs that were given to me when I lived with my aunt, so going to school was challenging. I had a total of three pair of pants and a hand full of shirts to wear to school and my mother made sure they were clean and ironed. Everything was on rotation. What I wore Monday through Wednesday, would be rotated to Thursday and Friday. Sometimes my mother would go to the welfare office to get clothes. They had a room filled with clothing and people were allowed to come and get whatever they wanted. Although the clothes were free, the idea of having to go there seemed to dampen my mother's spirit. This was a woman who had it all at one point. She had a home that she cleaned often, children that she adored and money to buy whatever she wanted. This was a very humbling experience for her. I learned how to take care of things and to this day I have an appreciation for that skill.

Everywhere I went in this small town, kind hearted people seemed to be plentiful. The principal at the elementary school knew that most of the families were very poor and he made a point of making sure all of the children had the opportunity to eat breakfast and lunch. It didn't matter how late students arrived, you had to eat and they fed us very well! My first day of school was difficult for about an hour. I cried when my mother left me in the room with all of these strangers, but they were different. They were nice! They understood why I was scared and they took me by the hand and made me feel comfortable and I ended up having a good day. I was also placed in the right grade! Wow! My mother actually knew how old I was! I was in the second grade and it was great! I discovered I could read and write. I was making A's! I didn't know what to do with that letter because I didn't have "A" as one of my initials! This was new for me! My teacher who is deceased now, was Mrs. S. She was a very sophisticated lady and she had very high expectations for her students. I was reading so well and because of that Mrs. S. allowed me to be the narrator for the Black History Program. I couldn't believe it and my mother was so proud. I even read the Emancipation Proclamation. I could read!!! I wasn't dumb after all!!! GOD was and is so good!!! HE gave me time to be a child again and

I was thriving. Mrs. S. cared about her students and she was able to pull the best out of us if we were willing and I was. She also had a **STRAP** and was not afraid to use it if students needed a little motivation to do their homework. It was great! I was blossoming and lacking the material things didn't matter much anymore. It didn't matter that I only had three pair of pants, a few tops and one pair of shoes. It didn't matter that sometimes we only had one box of spaghetti to eat (three adults and five children needing to eat). We learned how to appreciate different types of sandwiches like ketchup sandwiches, mayonnaise sandwiches, egg sandwiches, sandwich-spread sandwiches, sugar sandwiches, bread on bread sandwiches and molasses sandwiches — it was good!!! It didn't matter that we had no indoor plumbing. It didn't matter about the cold, cold winters and being able to see the ground from the peephole in the floor. **It didn't matter! I was happy and poor at the same time!!! I was content! I was free!** It felt so good, because we rarely heard from my father and when we did, it was over the phone. I was normal!!!

A few months later, we had to leave Mutt-Dear's home. We moved in with my maternal grandmother. I don't know what changed her mind, but I guess seeing someone else take your daughter and grandchildren in, makes room for conviction and repentance. It was crowed to say the least because of the number of people having to live in a three bedroom apartment. This was something else I had to adjust to. By this time, I had gotten used to living without the "lessons" from my father because my brother and I rarely saw him. I wondered if he had changed and if it would be different when we saw him again. He would tell us that he loved us and occasionally we would visit our grandparents and of course see him. My father ended up living in his hometown for a while and during that time he had gotten an apartment. He wanted us to see where he lived and of course as children, living in something new without a crowd of people in the same house was just great. I was developing early, so I didn't look like the average ten-year-old. Most ten-year-olds didn't have what I had or at least they didn't have as much as I had. My self-esteem was intact and my grades were fine. I had learned to take the initiative with my homework because my teachers whipped students who did not study. I remember receiving a paddling because I didn't know my "two time tables". Today they are called multiplication tables and I am sure they were called multiplication tables back then. After the paddling, I gained an appreciation for studying because the teachers did not play.

The new apartment was bittersweet. I was happy for my father, but as we walked through the apartment, I could feel the atmosphere change. A part of me was hoping and praying that things would be different. It had been some time since we had the opportunity to visit with him alone or at least away from my aunts' house. I had gotten used to being happy with the life I was living. I enjoyed being a little girl. My mother was struggling to take care of us and I was trying to be the best little girl I could be. I didn't talk back. I helped with my sister and brothers. I was receiving good grades. I couldn't control the way my body was developing, but I was hoping that no one would notice, and no one did, at least I thought no one did. But there was one — my father. He ignored the other things that I was good at and decided that he had to be satisfied! He didn't care. It was about what he wanted and not how it was affecting me.

I had a cousin who was a few years older than me and she was not afraid to tell you where to go and how to get there if you know what I mean. If you needed help getting where she told you to go, she was not afraid to assist you, so it was best that you use the common sense God gave you if you didn't want her to put her fist upside your head. She was nice like that, very helpful. She was just like her father. My uncle who was the "man of the house." That was her father and she was his daughter in every sense of the word. She was my friend and I thought she was fantastic. Whenever the opportunity presented itself, I would ask her if she wanted to spend the night with us. I would tell her to ask my father if she could spend the night because I wanted him to tell her whether it was all right or not. It is hard to say, "No" to someone when they are looking at you. When he would say, "Yes", I would be so happy. It was like Christmas. I celebrated silently because I knew that he wouldn't be able to do much to me. When she would sleep over, I'd try to sleep close to the edge of the bed making sure there was not enough room for him or sleep between my brother and my cousin thinking that this would save me from his abuse, but it didn't. He would move my brother in order to get behind me and then place his private part in my underwear while my cousin and brother slept near me. I would try to move away, but he would tighten his grip around my waist so that I couldn't get up. I can't really explain how it feels to be violated, but I can say it is a traumatic experience because you don't understand why it's happening. It is difficult to process.

I couldn't figure out what kind of man this was? To me, he was disgusting not fit to be called dad or father. He was teaching me remember. He would say, "I love you." I began to wonder why love hurt so much. I didn't want love, at least not that way. What happened to the singing and dancing we did when I was younger, was that a lie? Did he care about his daughter then, or was it a joke to him? What happened? Why was this happening all over again? What did I do to deserve this? What was the purpose for this and what exactly was I supposed to remember? I had no plans to do anything with what he was trying to teach me. Why would I want to destroy another person the way he was destroying me? Heartless!!!!

CHAPTER 4

*Scripture: Isaiah 54:17-No weapon
formed against thee shall prosper;
and every tongue that shall rise
against thee in judgment thou shalt
condemn. This is the heritage of
the servants of The Lord, and their
righteousness is of Me, saith the Lord.*

I was able to keep my grades up because I didn't
want to get a paddling from my teachers. I
couldn't tell them what was happening because I felt
all teachers were like the teachers from first grade.
My mother was still struggling, but she managed
to move into an apartment and it was much
better. She was receiving government assistance;
working at a convenience store part-time; and
working for my aunt on weekends in order to take
care of us. Meanwhile, my father decided to move
to Tennessee, so it was only during the summer
breaks or holidays that we would visit him. One
summer, my brother and I visited my father and
at the time he was renting a house. He worked
during the day and arrangements were made
for my brother and me to stay with a baby-sitter.

The baby-sitter was the wife of one of my father's friends from his hometown and they had two young sons. I will call the baby-sitter Mrs. B. Mrs. B had a job and she would have to leave two hours before my dad got off work. If her mother-in-law could not stay with us, her husband would keep us until my father arrived. For weeks things were fine even though I would have preferred to be at my cousin's house playing with them. One day the four of us, my brother, me and their two sons, were taking a nap and I woke up before the boys. Mr. B was sitting on the couch watching television and out of nowhere tells me to come here. I couldn't believe what I was hearing. My heart started racing and my breathing was shallow. I looked at him for a moment and because I had been raised to obey my elder's, I got up and walked over to him. He started unbuttoning my blouse and he said, "All I want to do is look." I was so scared. I didn't understand why it was necessary for him to look. What was he looking for! I had what looked like knobs on my chest! What was the purpose?! He along with my father were sick in the head and the heart! When he was finished looking, he closed my blouse and told me I could lay back down on the floor with the boys. I wanted to leave, but it wasn't time for my father to get off work. Why was this happening to me? I was a child! What kind of people could do this! I know — disgusting people!!

All I wanted was a father who treated me like a daughter. During the school year, I would be hoping that things would be different when I saw my father. Maybe he would realize what he was doing and stop teaching me things I didn't want to know! I dreamed of having a normal childhood and a father-daughter relationship that was filled with love and fun, but each time I was disappointed. If I told my mother I didn't want to go to visit my father, she would want to know why and because I didn't want to lie to her, I went along with the program. I was holding on and it had nothing to do with me and my ability, but GOD was keeping me. HE is powerful!

The school year had ended and I had completed the fifth grade. We were excited about the summer break and my brother and I went to visit my father again for summer vacation. He had an apartment, but it looked like an extended stay hotel room. I was now a sixth grader inside of a body that looked like someone in high school. Would this be the summer that I could relax and be a child? No abuse? I wondered and hoped. Well, as usual, he was not ready to treat me like his little girl and that was a shame. He could not see me.

He didn't abuse me every night, but at least once a week, he used my body to satisfy his sick and disgusting needs. I didn't know when I could relax and just breathe because he didn't tell me when he would be using me. He didn't care about my little brother being in the room, so I would have to put him to sleep first. There were times when he would try to wake up and I would pat him until he went back to sleep with my father naked in front of me. No child should have to go through this. Why couldn't I have my childhood? I realized there was nothing I could do to avoid my father, so my focus turned to my brother. The most important thing to me was my brother. I had to protect him from my father by making sure he did not disturb him. I did not want my dad to spank him just for being a child. I was being punished enough for both of us. My father would say, "Put it where you want it." I would push it off of me. He would ignore what I wanted and continue doing what he wanted and how he wanted. He would say, "Put it where you want it." I would push it off again. He refused to get the message and the message was I didn't want it on me!

My father had a habit of rubbing the tip of my left thumb whenever we were in the car. I couldn't stand it because I didn't want him touching me. I came up with a way to keep this from happening. I would dig in my nose and flick the boogers out of the window so if he rubbed my thumb, he would touch the left overs. I know it sounds disgusting, but I had to have control of something that involved my body. This would make him so angry and he would order me to stop! It disgusted him and I didn't care. Isn't it ironic? I felt the same way about what he had done to me, the only difference is I couldn't order him to stop.

I had to find something to focus on in order to keep from speaking or crying, so I would turn my head towards the television and I would keep my head in that position until it was time for me to clean myself up. I would tell him that I had to use the bathroom and he would allow this, but then he would come into the bathroom with me, position me across his lap and tote me back to the bed. I would turn my head towards the television again to remove myself from what was happening. I didn't care about the show that was on because I would have a blank stare on my face, it was almost like I was in a peaceful place even though my body was in the middle of chaos! It was my way of escape. He would try to kiss me, but again this is not something that wanted or needed to learn and definitely not from my father! I would lock my lips and teeth together and use every muscle in my body to keep his tongue out of my mouth. I had to do this until he stopped trying. When he was finished, I had to clean myself up and he would act as if nothing had happened. He didn't change his personality; he didn't feel guilty, but acted in his normal way. I couldn't understand how he could get up the next day and act like he was the responsible father. He wanted me to smile and act like life was great. He would even tell me that he was "scoping" me out which meant he had been watching me. He could sense that something was wrong. He even wanted me to tell him what was wrong. What kind of question and request was that?! Didn't he know what he was doing was wrong! Of course he did or he wouldn't have asked! I had to teach myself how to put on a "happy go jolly" show on the outside while sad and miserable on the inside. I taught myself well. I taught myself how to lie about how I really felt. It was exhausting. I came to the conclusion that this was the way my life was going to be. I couldn't even tell my mother. I was upset with her because it seemed as if she had more time for other things. I knew she had to work, but she had time for her boyfriend, so why didn't she have time for me? She didn't even have time to tell me about the menstrual cycle. After we returned home from our visit with my father, I had my first cycle. I thought I was bleeding to death! I was screaming for my aunts to come and help me and when they realized what was happening, they told me it was nothing and asked if my mother had told me about the cycle — of course not! If she had, I wouldn't have been screaming for dear life!

My sixth grade year was a turning point for me. Life was not fair. I felt like I was all alone in the world. There were people around me, but I was alone. I was struggling and hurting on the inside and no one seemed to care. We would go to church occasionally with my Uncle J and his family, but the only thing I knew about JESUS was salvation. I received my salvation when I was much younger so there wasn't much JESUS could do for me now, at least this is what I thought. I noticed that my friends had boyfriends and I was wondering how you could get one of those things — a boyfriend.

So, I decided to observe the actions of the girls and find out how they related to boys. This was not included in what my father was trying to "teach" me. I noticed that some boys looked very good. The older boys looked nice and no one mentioned anything about age or grade restrictions. My mother was too busy to discuss these things with me and I was curious. At the end of my sixth grade year, I had sex (fornicated) with a ninth grader and as a result, lost my virginity and became pregnant. Losing my virginity was almost as worse as being sexually abused by my father. I didn't tell anyone that I was pregnant.

Before visiting my father for the summer, I was allowed to spend a few weeks with my mother's sister and during that time I pretended to have my cycle. I went through the whole routine of wearing pads, wrapping them up after each use and throwing them in the trash. I did this for a week. Shortly after, I left my aunt's house and returned home because my father had arrived and my brother and I were allowed to spend a portion of the summer break with him. By this time, he was living with a girlfriend. She was nice, but she had a job and there were times when he would arrive home before her and I would be sitting in the corner of the couch wishing that she would hurry home because I didn't know what kind of plans he had that involved abusing me. During that summer, my father's oldest sister was killed in a car accident and we attended the funeral service.

If you paid attention to me, you could tell I was pregnant because my stomach was larger, but no one noticed.

A few days later, we returned to my dad's home. I thought everything was going pretty good until someone told my mother that I was pregnant. My mother, being concerned, contacted my father and told him that there was a possibility that I was pregnant and that he needed to take me to the doctor. He was so angry! I was trying to figure out why. This is what he was training me for was it not?! He told me that he would knock the baby through my backend and that is saying it lightly and I believed he would hurt me and my baby, but his girlfriend was trying to assure me that he would not do that—I believed what he said. My little brother was sitting beside me on the couch and he was so quiet. We had never seen that side of my father and it scared us. I know my brother was confused and if the corner of the couch had a hole in it large enough for us, we would have been through it. They were brutal, the words he was saying.

He took me to the doctor and the doctor confirmed that I was indeed pregnant. The doctor told me to go out of the room so he could talk things over with my father. He supposedly told my father that if I had my baby, I would die because I was so young (eleven years old). The doctor called me into the room and asked me if I was going to have the baby? I was standing beside my father while he sat in the chair. He didn't look up at me when the doctor asked the question. I looked down at my father and the only thing I could remember was what he said he would do to my baby the night before. The thought of my child going through any harm at the hands of my father was not an option. I had to protect my baby and the only way my eleven year old mind could figure out how to do it was to have an abortion. We returned to the apartment and it was still early. My brother was at my uncle's house and my father's girlfriend was at work, so we were alone in the apartment. I was so scared, almost terrified because I didn't know what he was going to do. I sat on the couch in the corner wishing that I could just sink to the bottom of it and be outside. I sat there quietly while he was in the bedroom. I didn't know what he was thinking, but I heard my name being called. As a child who obeys, I got up and went to see what he wanted. He told me that he did not believe the doctor knew what he was talking about when he said I was pregnant and instructed me to pull my panties down and get on the bed so that he could check me. **He was a MECHANIC!!! What was he supposed to be checking and how would he know what it was if he found it!!!** I did as he instructed and he opened my legs and stuck his finger inside my vagina to check me. I was terrified. I didn't know what he was going to do next. I didn't want to make any sudden moves. I wanted to be as quiet as possible. I was pregnant and you can't get someone who is already pregnant, pregnant again! What would he do to me?! **I wanted to get up! That's all I wanted!** While he was checking me, all I could do was ask for help. Some people may think the only way you can get a prayer through is by opening your mouth and praying out loud, but I am able to testify that that is not true. I KNOW THE LORD HEARD MY CRY! HE KNOWS OUR THOUGHTS AND HE KNOWS WHAT IS IN OUR HEARTS! HE IS THE ONLY ONE WHO COULD HAVE MOVED ON MY BEHALF THE WAY HE DID! When my father finished checking me, he stood up and told me to put my panties back on and he left me alone for that day. Later that evening, we went to my uncle's house to pick up my brother. I placed myself in the corner of the couch and tried to be invisible. I spoke only when I was spoken to. My father was fuming. He told my uncle and his wife about my condition and while he was talking with my uncle, I asked my aunt if I could play with my baby cousin, but my father told me, "No." That irritated my aunt, so she took my brother and my cousins to the back bedroom. I didn't move a muscle! My father told me to go to the back and when I entered my aunt's room, she was watching a western, so I sat at the foot of the bed. While sitting there, the only thing I could think about was what my father was going to do to me. I needed help!

My aunt was so nice and when she felt things were not fair, you could tell. She always made my brother and I feel at home. If she took her children to the movie, my brother and I were included along with her sister's children. If we were hungry, she fed us. So I was comfortable with her. We were watching the western or at least she was. When I stopped focusing on my father, I began to relax and I heard a voice say, "Tell her." It was very clear and it was like someone was speaking directly into my ear, so I looked behind me at my aunt to see if it was her talking to me, but she had not said anything. I couldn't believe what I was hearing. I turned back around facing the television and the voice said, "Tell her, you can trust her." I sat there for a moment and then I turned in my aunt's direction and whispered, "Daddy is messing with me." She looked at me as if she needed me to say it again. So I said it again, "Daddy is messing with me." I was waiting on her reaction. I didn't know if she was going to tell my father what I told her. I just didn't know what was going to happen. She started talking and after I realized what she was doing, I was hopeful that things were going to work out. She was giving me a way of escape! Freedom! She was trying to help me! She told me to ask my father if I could spend the night at their house. If he agreed, she would take me to a safe house the next morning. I went into the living room where my father and uncle were sitting and asked my father if I could spend the night and he said no! I almost lost it—on the inside. It took every ounce of strength to go back into the bedroom and tell my aunt what he said. I thought the nightmare would never end! I began to cry because it seemed hopeless, BUT THE LORD WAS IN THAT ROOM AND I DIDN'T EVEN KNOW THAT HE COULD DO THAT. YOU KNOW HE ALWAYS HAS A RAM IN THE BUSH! HE gave my aunt a new plan. She told me to go home with my father and she would pick me up on her lunch break the following day. At this point, I was sobbing because I knew I had to leave with my father. She reassured me that it would be all right. My father took us back to the apartment and my brother and I went to bed.

The next day it seemed as if my aunt's lunch break would never come. It was important for her to get me out of the house before my father or his girlfriend returned home. Finally, there was a knock at the door, and it was my aunt! She took me and my brother to the home of a woman I will call Mrs. D. Mrs. D. was something like a foster parent. I had to stay with her during the day while my aunt worked. Mrs. D. opened her home to me. She taught me how to crochet and she fed me. I sat at the table with her and her children and they nurtured me. She was beautiful on the outside and the inside and greatly appreciated to this day. I had to tell the social workers what happened and as I was talking with them, it was as if I was talking about something that happened to a friend or someone else. I was emotionless. I didn't cry. I focused on the little crocheted piglet that Mrs.

D. had given me and answered the questions they asked. I didn't even look at them and it was almost as if I was ashamed of what had happened to me; like it was my fault. I didn't want my father to be in trouble, I just wanted him to stop abusing me.

The police were sent to the location where my father worked and they confronted him. He denied everything and they told him he had to take us back to Mississippi as soon as possible or go to jail. My father's girlfriend didn't believe I knew what I was talking about. She felt that it was impossible for me to know about sex (fornication). I did know what it was and I knew it because my father had been abusing me since I was five! I knew what it was!

My appointment for the abortion had been scheduled and my father had to take me to the abortion clinic to have the procedure done. When he came to pick me up, he didn't show any anger towards me and that surprised me. I didn't know how to process it because that is not how he acted when he found out. When we entered the abortion clinic, it was filled with women and girls and I assumed they were there for the same reason. My father helped me fill out the paperwork and all we had to do then was wait until my name was called. I sat quietly in the waiting room—almost numb. Prior to making the decision to have the abortion, I could feel my baby move, but on the day of the abortion, it didn't move. I was just helpless and hopeless. I felt isolated and confused about everything and on top of that, I had no one to talk to about my feelings. I had no feelings I guess, just numb. The idea that I wouldn't have my baby combined with the thoughts of everything that had taken place up to that point, was too overwhelming and I had to adjust to what was going on. If a person is numb, does that mean they have peace? I don't know but if that was the case, I didn't know where the peace came from during the storm, but I know now THE LORD was with me. It was like I was staring at a wall expecting something to happen, but it didn't. Is that peace? That's how it was for me at that time in the abortion clinic.

They called me back and I had to undress and put on the gown they provided. When it was time for the actual procedure, they rolled me into a room that was very cold. The walls were white and void of pictures. The doctor was straight to the point. He explained what was about to happen. When he turned on the machine, it made a loud noise and within minutes — it was over. Just like that, it was over. I had given these people permission to kill my baby. Was this the only way to protect my baby from my father, I didn't know, but at time in my eleven year old mind, I could not allow the same abuse that happened to me, happen to my child. Say what you will, but GOD has forgiven me and my father.

They rolled me back into the recovery room and later released me. I was worn out and emotionally drained. All I wanted to do was rest. **I was in shock. I had given these people permission to kill my baby! What had I done! All of the condemnation came crashing down on me and it didn't matter that I was eleven because I had to mature emotionally very fast! When would this be over?** I didn't have much to say to my father on the way back to his home which was an hour away from the abortion clinic. I think he was happy because his little girl was no longer pregnant. I was so tired on our way back and he noticed that I was because he questioned me about it. I told him that I was sleepy, so he told me that I could lay down and get some sleep. Because of my size, I could get into a tight fetal position on the front seat. When I laid down, my bottom was towards my door on the passenger side turned away from him. Because I had an abortion, I had to wear a pad because of the bleeding. As I was dozing off, I noticed that he was reaching over my shoulder to put his hand on my bottom and I immediately sat up! **What was he thinking! I just had an abortion and they killed my baby! I was so angry and different now! I had nothing to lose and if it was necessary for me to fight my father, I was prepared to do so! Yes, this eleven year old child was going to fight her father if he tried anything else with me! I didn't care anymore and that was a dangerous place to be!**

When we arrived at his girlfriend's apartment, I went to my room and asked THE LORD TO FORGIVE ME AND TAKE CARE OF MY BABY. I cried every day for three days straight asking THE LORD THE SAME THING EACH DAY. It may seem strange to those who want to judge me, but I knew enough to know that I had killed my baby. I cried and prayed and cried and prayed. I told THE LORD how sorry I was and after a few days, I gained a sense of peace. Where did the peace come from? It came from THE LORD. *Philippians 4:7 says, "And the peace of God, which transcends all understanding, will guard your hearts and your minds in Christ Jesus." 1 John 1:9 says, "If we confess our sins, He is faithful and just to forgive us our sins, and to cleanse us from all unrighteousness."*

I was so happy just because of the idea of being back in my mother's care. A few weeks later, my father brought me and my brother home to our mother. When we arrived, my mother had a man living with her. My mother's boyfriend told my father that he could not see us anymore because of what I had told the social workers. My brother was being punished because of what I had done. He didn't understand why he couldn't see our father anymore. My intention was to get him to stop abusing me, but I didn't know that we would be forbidden to see him. My mother hugged us and took our belongings inside. She never asked me anything about what had taken place. It seemed as if I received more sympathy from her boyfriend. He was the same boyfriend from Duncan. I needed my mother. She is the one

I wanted, but she wasn't prepared to deal with the situation from an emotional standpoint. I guess it was difficult because not only did she find out her eleven year old daughter was pregnant and had an abortion, but that her husband had been sexually abusing her child for years and she didn't know it. That would be an overwhelming situation for any mother, but I was only concerned about me at the time and what I wanted and needed. To me, it was like being rejected by my mother and another indication that I needed to suck it up and get over it.

I visited my paternal grandparents shortly after coming home to my mother. Of course my father was there and for the most part my cousins and some of the family still loved me and treated like I was family and not the enemy. You could tell that they were curious about things and if I had opened up and shared what happened, they would have listened. There were those who looked at me strange. They didn't say anything about what happened and I knew they didn't believe me. Because it was rather cold outside, my cousins and I decided it was time to warm up, so we went to visit my grandmother. As we were trying to get warm, I noticed my grandmother staring at me and all of a sudden she said, "How could you say those things about your father?" "You shouldn't have said those things about your father." Every muscle in my body got weak and all I could do was stand there and stare at her because I didn't know how to respond. My cousin saw my reaction and quickly grabbed my arm and said, "Let's get out of here because this woman is crazy!" As we were walking out, I began to cry. Hadn't I been through enough! When was it going to be over! Why can't I just be normal! My cousin told me not to pay attention to my grandmother, but it was too late. My grandmother had already done more damage to my heart and my self-worth. It was my fault that my family was scarred and relationships were divided. Everything was my fault! I was so ashamed. Where could I hide?

When I returned to my home, my Daddy Lonnie was worried about me because he and my Momma Bessie were told I could have died. I didn't want them to worry any longer, so I went to see them. When I got there, he was on oxygen and barely breathing and my Momma Bessie said, "Look at what you did." I looked and I thought to myself, I almost killed my Daddy Lonnie! I didn't intend for any of this to happen! I only wanted my father to leave me alone! The weight, the shame, and the guilt that fell on me when she said that was so overwhelming. All I wanted to do was make him feel better. What could I do to make it right? Everything pointed to me; it was my fault! It was as if I was the perpetrator, but I was the victim! I wanted to be normal and happy, but I was persecuted by the people I thought would have compassion for me. Is this why most people (adults, teens, children, boys and girls) don't tell anyone that they are being abused?! It's not fair! As the days went by, my Daddy Lonnie seemed to get better because he was able to see that I was fine and not dying.

School was about to start in a few weeks and I would be going into the seventh grade. I knew that I wouldn't be seeing my father much and I wouldn't be visiting my grandparents either, so I had to find a way to preserve something that represented the good in me and what I considered to be pretty, but I couldn't think of anything. I would sit in the living room and try to think of something that was pretty about myself day in and day out, but I noticed that life was just happening around me and no one seemed to noticed the fact that I was about to check out mentally. I was abused; I had an abortion; I disgraced my father and my family; I almost killed my Daddy Lonnie whom I loved so dearly; I was nothing... Hopeless, helpless and full of shame—nothing! I just sat in the living room waiting to find something pretty and then I heard a voice say, "Your name is pretty." My name is Chywanda Faye. My father and other relatives called me Faye. The only time my mother would call me Chywanda was if I didn't respond to Faye. So, I decided that the abuse and the abortion happened to Faye. Faye was the angry, ugly, disgusting part of me and Chywanda was the pretty part of me. My classmates and teachers called me Chywanda. They did not know about what happened and they didn't need to know. Some people may think that this was insane, but I wanted to live and enjoy my life. I wanted my life back!

I entered the seventh grade angry, mixed up, and confused, but because of my name, I learned to act like nothing was wrong. I had to learn things on my own. It was trial and error with me. If I had to lose something in the process or sacrifice myself, I did it. If there was another way, no one mentioned or showed it to me. I wanted attention. I wanted to be loved and feel as if I belonged to someone. I was in survival mode. Everything I knew up to this point was learned the wrong way and I didn't know the right way. I decided that I didn't want to have sex (fornicate) anymore, so I stopped hanging around the "in crowd." By this time, I was fully developed and I tried to conceal the shape of my body the best way I could, but it was difficult. I would wear big flannel shirts and other baggy clothes because I didn't want to draw attention to myself. I didn't want anyone saying anything to me or make a pass at me. One day I was returning home from the corner store and a young man who was the brother of one of my classmates told me that if I came outside again, he would rape me. I didn't understand what was wrong with me! I didn't have to do anything or say anything and these people, **disgusting people** wanted to abuse me. Where could I go to be free? I wondered why he would say this. What had I done to him? I didn't even know his name. It was my fault. I came to the conclusion that it was my body.

From that point on, I could not look at my body. I could see myself, but in a distorted way. I did this for years and I can't even remember how my breast looked without clothing on because I did not look at myself. I did not want to see what my father saw. My body was the cause of everything that had gone wrong in my life. This is what I believed. I couldn't tell my mother about the pressure I was feeling and I was afraid to tell her what the young man told me so, to keep my mind occupied, I would either read through the encyclopedia or just watch television. I was extra careful about going to the store. I'd go with someone and if I had to go alone, I would make sure no one was standing in front of the building. I also stayed close to our apartment building whenever I was outside. My favorite sport at the time was kickball and my aunts, cousins, and neighbors would come out and we would have so much fun. It was during these times that I didn't have to think about the pain I was feeling. I felt a sense of relief even if it was for a short period of time.

I managed to get through the seventh grade. My Daddy Lonnie passed away and that was a painful experience for me. Losing someone I loved and who loved me was difficult. There were times when I would be walking or riding my bike and I would see a man who looked like my Daddy Lonnie and I would race to see if it was him, but then I'd realize it was someone who resembled him. That happened several times and I guess it was because I didn't want to believe he was dead. Having to let go was the hardest thing. He was my father in every sense of the word except biologically.

CHAPTER 5

Scripture: Psalm 25:7-Remember not the sins of my youth, nor my transgressions: according to thy mercy remember thou me for thy goodness sake, O LORD.

High school was a different ball game. I had to learn things as I went along with the baggage of my past — the Faye things. At times I would cry, but I couldn't talk to my mother. Being a single mother with five children was a challenge and I guess she was doing her best. We had moved to a different location in town during my eighth grade year and she had a live-boyfriend along with the hopes and dreams (lies) that normally never come true when a man is living off of what you bring in. I would watch my mother and she would get frustrated at times, because of how her life was going. My siblings and I wanted more from our mother. We hungered for quality time, but she felt that because she was at home sitting on the couch or in the bedroom with her boyfriend, we should be satisfied, but we were not. It was as if she had to make a choice between her man and her children and we ended up getting the short end of the stick. I would watch my mother because I couldn't talk to her. She would get angry and give me the opinion that she felt I should have and would miss the whole point of why I needed her to listen to me. She made the mistake of looking at me in terms of how teens with a normal upbringing were acting and behaving, but the other teens had not experienced what I had experienced. I didn't feel like a regular teen! What was that! My happy childhood was snatched away at the age of five, but she couldn't or didn't want to understand that. I was losing respect for her.

I watched how she handled herself with her children and with her male companion. She didn't even realize she was grooming her children. She was still married to my father and living with this man as if he was her husband. From watching my mother, I learned that there were really three types of men. Husbands were not necessary. The first type of man was one who didn't mind issuing out his money. If a bill needed to be paid, he would provide the resources. This made him feel like he was in charge of the relationship. This man also required certain things. When he was coming over, the bedroom had to be clean, the body had to be clean and food had to be prepared. This man wouldn't be spending the night because nine times out of ten, he was married. The second man was someone who had potential. He was working and had a good head on his shoulders. He wanted to do something with his life and he wanted a woman who was willing to be patient enough to work with him. This was the live-in boyfriend. What the children wanted was not important and what was best for the children was not considered. The third man looks good and may or may not have a job. Having a job is not important in this case. This is the man you would share a few laughs and a dance or two with at the club, which would lead to an attraction between the two of you. Because of this attraction, it would be all right for him to stop by and have sex (adultery), but he would have to leave the next day.

My mother tried to take care of her needs and fill the void in her heart, but she sacrificed herself and the relationship with her children in the process. Is this the way she wanted her life to be, of course not, but she was trying to live the best way she knew how. If only she had known JEHOVAH JIRAH (THE PROVIDER). **THE LORD IS THE PROVIDER OF EVERYTHING WE NEED. However, so many single mothers don't even know HIM. They know of HIM, but they don't have an intimate relationship with JESUS. She knew about HIM, but she didn't know HIM. When you read HIS WORD, you get to know HIM and when you hear things contrary to what HE SAID IN HIS WORD, you will have the wisdom to know the difference. So when a man comes to you and say I can take care of you if we move in or if we get to know each other better (fornicate),** you can decline his offer because you know your **HEAVENLY FATHER HAS YOU COVERED! HE WILL SEND YOU A HUSBAND; THE ONE HE HAS CHOSEN ESPECIALLY FOR YOU! HE LOVES YOU AND YOU HAVE TO TRUST HIM, SO JUST SURRENDER EVERYTHING TO HIM AND WATCH HIM WORK ON YOUR BEHALF.**

After watching my mother for a period of time, I decided I didn't need money. I didn't have a financial problem. All I wanted was someone to listen. I wanted to know that someone cared about how I felt and what I was experiencing. Having sex (fornicating) was not a part of my agenda, but if it was required, I considered it. I went to church, but like most teenagers, I didn't know JESUS and when you don't have a relationship with HIM, you will make mistakes and my mistakes would have consequences.

In high school, I was fairly quiet. I didn't approach boys, but every now and then one would get enough nerve to approach me. I was told I looked mean. I wasn't mean; I just didn't have a lot to smile about. In high school, I had two serious relationships that are worth mentioning. I didn't know that having sex when you are not married was fornication, a sin. I didn't know that I was committing a sin. It wasn't discussed that way in my family. As a matter of fact, for most of my family, it was a way of life. I didn't know that I was to *flee fornication/sexual immorality. All other sins a man commits are outside his body, but he who sins sexually sins against his own body. Do you not know that your body is a temple of the Holy Spirit, who is in you, whom you have received from God? You are not your own; you were bought at a price. Therefore honor God with your body. (1 Corinthians 6:18-20)*

The first serious relationship took place during my ninth grade year. I will not use his name because the book is not about him. It is about the decisions I made, the lessons I learned, and how THE LORD kept me during this process. The young man was on the basketball team in high school when we met and he was a character. He was tall, nice looking, and a senior. He began flirting with me so innocently and I thought it was funny. One night we had a basketball event at the high school and when I arrived, the gym was practically empty, so I left early. As I was walking home, he caught up with me and walked me the rest of the way and that was the beginning of what my ninth grade mind thought was a beautiful relationship. We had things to talk about and he seemed to care about me. My mother, with all of the things she had to deal with was a smart woman when she needed to be. She could smell "no good" when it came around me, but it was difficult for her to smell "no good" when the scent came around her. She told me that this young man was no good. That he only wanted one thing and of course, I didn't believe her. She asked if I was having sex and I told her no. I was lying. Yes, I lied to my mother. Why? For years, I wanted to talk to my mother about these issues and was not able to do so because she was busy — she didn't have time. I felt it was too late to have a mother-daughter talk and I didn't believe she cared. I didn't respect her opinion or her advice. The only thing important to me at the time was how I felt when I was with him. I enjoyed his company. Everything was fine until I found out he was cheating on me. Why couldn't he just be honest? If fornication was the objective, why not say so in the beginning? Give a girl a chance to make an honest decision. The process is simple. Just say, "Hi, my name is EFG and I want to fornicate with you." The answer will probably be no, but at least everyone will be on an even playing field. He was very clever. Whenever I would ask about the girl, he would say, "I broke up with her, but she doesn't want to break up." What did that mean? I didn't know what to do with that information. I was beginning to feel as if I was being used and I didn't like it. I didn't want to talk to my mother about it, and I was tired of games, so the cycle began; we would break up and get back together and so on and so forth.

I became ill one year and was out of school for almost a week and he came over because he was concerned. My mother of course became sick to her stomach when she found out he was in the living room. He pretended to be concerned and he even began to cry and I just looked at him. I was trying to make things difficult for him and we started the relationship again shortly after that. I did care about him, but I didn't like his games. One night as we were walking home, the young lady that he supposedly broke up with drove up and she started to cry because he was trying to explain our relationship. He decided that I should walk home alone and he got into the car with her and they rode off. I was very, very, very upset! He had hurt me for the last time! So I thought.

I became pregnant with his child and I was trying to keep it a secret, but my mother was so into her children in a way that I didn't realize. She may not have been there for quality time, but she could tell if there were changes taking place. One day I was standing in the doorway looking out and she walked through the living room. She stopped and asked, "Are you pregnant? I said, "Yes." She said, "Are you going to have the baby?" I said, "Yes." That was the end of the conversation. When I was about five months pregnant, he (my baby's father) came over for a visit. He had graduated from high school and the plans he had did not include us. We were both young and he was not prepared to be a father. I came to accept it. You can't force people to do things they don't want to do. I had to grow up whether I wanted to or not.

Being pregnant with my son allowed me to view my body differently. It was during my pregnancy that I began to pay attention. My body was changing and I began to appreciate how I looked. I could actually stand in front of a mirror and not be ashamed of the way I looked. It was an interesting experience. I think I was amazed at how large my midsection was getting and all I could do was stare at it and rub it because my baby was growing on the inside of me. I loved him before he was born. I had my son in 1984 and he was the best thing for me because I had someone else to focus on. Getting pregnant in high school is an experience I wouldn't advise. The ridicule and looks from teachers, the strained and broken relationships with friends, and the parents who tend to keep their children away from you can be harsh punishment. I decided I wouldn't have any more children until I was married and I didn't.

After I had my son, I knew I would have to make changes and I knew that being on welfare was not the best thing for me, so I got a job working at a local restaurant. This allowed me to take responsibility for my actions. I knew I had to lighten the burden for my mother and I also had to take care of my son. I was able to do that with a job that paid $3.25 per hour. I was so excited! Most juniors in high school didn't have a job, but I did. I remained in school after having my son and maintained a high GPA, but I learned that school was different for girls with babies. My classes were the same and my friends were the same, but most of my teachers had changed. They assumed I would drop out of high school and end up with a house filled with children by the age of twenty. I was not a lazy student before my pregnancy, but for most of my teachers, I had to prove myself worthy again to be considered a good student. My Home Economics, English, and French teachers did not change the way they treated me. They worked with me and made sure I received my make-up work. I had a male friend my mother referred to as "spaghetti" because he was so skinny. He was an honor roll student and he would sit in the class with me after school to make sure I completed my assignments. He was the best. I had another friend that I will call Mr. D. who was on the football team (the nicest guy to me), who was like my bodyguard. He would not allow me to walk home at night alone. If I went to the local restaurant to get something to eat after the game, he would walk me home and then walk back to the school or restaurant to be with his friends. He never disrespected me and he never asked for anything other than friendship. I believe THE LORD was showing me that all young men were not out to use me. THE LORD also began to change my relationship with my mother. She wasn't mean to me after I had my son, as a matter of fact, our conversations were much longer and I was gaining an appreciation for her advice. Unfortunately, I was still struggling with the advice she had about boys especially if they had their own car and was not hard on the eyes.

The period of time between my junior and senior year in high school was difficult. I was gradually dealing with my past and I was trying to handle motherhood along with school. My mother was very supportive and she took care of my son while I was at school and work. I was still longing for someone to love me and one day again I thought I had met him. I will not mention his name because it is about the decisions I made, the consequences and how THE LORD WAS THERE FOR ME. He was nice looking and spoiled and in the end a very cruel person. Of course I couldn't see this, but my mother could. The purpose of motherly advice is to keep you out of harm's way, but if you do not take heed to wise counsel, you will live to regret it and I did. Mother's don't want their daughters to experience the same pain and heartache they experienced, but when you are filled with pride, like I was, the only way the lesson will be learned is by going through it. This is what my mother would call "bought sense."

I didn't heed my mother's warning and that would turn out to be a big mistake. This young man played mind games and what that means is, he would test me to see where I was emotionally. If I was happy, he would bring me down and if I was down, he would bring me up and then drop me. He would say all of the right things to make me think the relationship was fine, but he would break up with me a week later. One weekend, we were both working the night shift at the local restaurant and because it was the weekend, all of the young ladies who were working, volunteered to leave early because business was slow. Well, I didn't leave because the only thing I would have done was go home and go to bed. I didn't want to do that. I was the only female working with all males. How cool was that! They treated me like I was their little sister, so I was fine. We were laughing and doing our jobs at the same time. The atmosphere was pleasant. My "boyfriend" didn't like it, so he decided to pull into the drive thru and end our relationship. Who does that?! I could not figure him out! It was an emotional roller coaster ride with this guy. He was the kind of person who would break up with you a few days before Christmas so he wouldn't have to buy you a gift. These are the kind of people who draw you in for the kill and all of the advice in the world couldn't tear you away from them. Once, he told me that I had to make a choice between him and my son. I looked at my child and I look at him and this is when I saw him for who he was! Was he crazy or just stupid?! Of course, I chose my baby! Let me give you some advice ladies. If you find yourself in a relationship that is off one week and on the next, listen to wise counsel and leave it off. It is a control play and if you fall for it they will have the control and don't choose a man over your children. If he is worth being with, he will want you and the children because you are a package deal.

All of the advice my mother tried to give wasn't enough. I wanted to be loved and I also wanted to be clean and pure, but how could that happen with dirty people in my life and a self-esteem level of zero. I didn't love myself but I wanted other people to love me and it doesn't work that way. He could see that I didn't love myself because if I did, he would not have been able to treat me the way he did. I was at fault. I wondered how my life was supposed to be because this was too much for one person to handle and it was not fair. I was hurt because I wanted someone in my life and I was tired of hurting. I was tired of trying to please people; I was tired of being treated like trash; I was just fed up with this life I was living! So, I decided that I would end it all! I knew my mother would take care of my son, so I left the house around nine o'clock one night determined to run into the first car I saw. I didn't care about their lives. I didn't care about how my family would feel. I was so focused. It was almost like I was possessed and under the control of something or someone who wanted me dead. I knew I would be able to complete my mission because there was always traffic in my neighborhood. I drove and drove and the roads were clear! I couldn't believe it! Where was everybody?! Didn't they know I was going to kill myself and I needed another car on the road to do it?! I heard a voice say, "Run into the poll." I didn't want to do that. I was determined to wait on the car, but there was no car to be found. I came to a stop sign and made a left turn. As I was doing so, I asked myself who was powerful enough to stop traffic? As soon as I had that thought, the answer came to mind and I said, "GOD!" As soon as I said HIS NAME, I saw a car coming my way.

It was too late! THE LORD STOPPED MY PLANS TO TAKE MY LIFE! I began to weep and I told HIM that HE would have to help me with this since HE stopped my plans. Yes, I was feeling sorry for myself. Today, I know that it was not my life to take because I didn't create it; however, at that time I didn't know that I was *"fearfully and wonderfully made and bought with a price." (Psalm 139:14; 1 Corinthians 6:20)* You see *"God so loved the world that He gave his only begotten Son. That whosoever believeth in Him should not perish, but have everlasting life." (John 3:16)* GOD LOVED YOU AND ME SO MUCH THAT **HE GAVE** AND **HE CREATED**, SO WE HAVE NO RIGHT TO TAKE WHAT HE HAS GIVEN. HE loves us and it is important for us to know this and not only know this but believe it and we can because it is the Truth!

During my senior year, I was a member of the National Honor Society and Vice-President of the Senior Class. I participated in the Ms. Zodiac Pageant and graduated with honors. I was ranked fourteen out of one hundred and six students. I was able to take care of my son with the help of my mother and pay for everything I needed my senior year except my prom dress. My aunt had it made for me. My father even bought me a car for graduation. It seemed as if I had it all, but I didn't. Have you ever met someone who looks good on the outside and it seems like they have it all together, but if you scratch the surface, you would find a hurt and wounded soul? That was me. After everything I had accomplished, I still felt alone, angry, and empty. I felt dirty and disgusting because I had reconciled that the abuse, the abortion, and everything that was in the baggage for "Faye", happened to me, Chywanda Faye. There was no one to talk to because everyone thought I was fine. I was a good manipulator and pretender. I needed to let it out! I needed someone to listen and pay attention, but there was no one I could trust. When you have been violated sexually, you need to know that there is someone who can relate to what you are feeling. Saying, "I understand how you are feeling," doesn't mean anything if you have not gone through similar situations. Sure you may be able to talk to a counselor for a week or two, but can they relate? I needed to talk to someone who could relate to the trauma and the shame that came with the abuse and the abortion. Most victims keep quiet for many reasons. Can they trust the person they are revealing things to? Will they get the help and support they need? Will they be blamed for what happened to them or will they be victimized all over again?! There has to be a way to heal without being traumatize all over again! Parents when your child tells you that someone touched, raped, or forced them to do things that they should not be doing, please believe them and do something about it. They need to know that they can get through this and they desperately need to know that JESUS loves them unconditionally. When you leave it up to the victims to heal themselves, they will not do it the way you think they should. Get them the help that is needed.

CHAPTER 6

Scripture: Psalm 27:1-THE LORD is my light and my salvation; whom shall I fear? THE LORD is the strength of my life; of whom shall I be afraid?

I moved to Tennessee when I was thirty-two. Years had passed and by the year 2000, I had been married and going through the process of getting a divorce. I wondered why my life was like this. Why a divorce? Why did my relationships with men end with so much pain? In 2000, I decided I needed to find out why, so I took the vow of celibacy. I needed to know what was wrong with me. I had three beautiful children. I had gone to college, graduated and started teaching and the primary reason for moving to Tennessee was due to the teacher salary. Yes, I came for the money. I taught at the high school and my children, the two youngest attended the elementary school next door. My oldest son was at the high school with me his last semester. When I moved, I didn't have the money to get a place for me and my children, so one of my cousins allowed us to live with him and his family for a month. For a month, I didn't attend church. It was not a concern for me at the time. I don't even think I asked my cousin about the church he attended. It was kind of strange because I always attended church before the move.

According to my Momma Bessie, I was baptized at the age of three and again when I was in elementary school, however, I don't remember being baptized at three and again in the second grade, but I didn't know the purpose. The only thing I knew about JESUS was HE died on the Cross and rose again and that HE was gone to prepare a place for us. I knew if you did not repent of your sins, you would go to hell. I also knew THE LORD WAS THE ALMIGHTY GOD AND that HE PARTED THE RED SEA. I saw that in a movie. I rarely ever read the BIBLE and I rarely saw people reading the BIBLE outside of church, so I thought I was fine. I was afraid of HIM. I thought HE was a GOD who punished and that was the only thing HE DID. Love was nowhere in the picture. I guess I was afraid of HIS wrath, because I didn't know about HIS GRACE AND MERCY. I longed to have a father who could love me without requiring me to suffer in the process. I would watch other father's with their daughters and find it hard to believe that nothing was going on. I thought all fathers were abusing their daughters and that there was a price for the smile that was on their faces.

After I moved into my own apartment, I asked my cousin about the church he attended. He told me the name, but I forgot what he said. I decided to ask him if I could go to church with him and his family and he told me I could. When we arrived, I noticed that the church was fairly large and it was packed. The people were standing and praising THE LORD and they even praised HIM without having to wait for instructions. I thought that was neat. I enjoyed myself. I visited the church a few more times with my children and began to feel condemned because I didn't know how to give to the church (tithe) and take care of my children, so I stopped going. I continued to struggle financially and in the meantime the church had changed locations and eventually placed a statue of liberation in the front lawn of the church. It looked just like the statue of liberty. I decided that I could not stay away from church any longer. Each time I visited, I enjoyed the services. I noticed that there was one thing that made this church different from those I had attended in the past. The people prayed in an unknown tongue. I had only heard someone speak this way once or twice before and I thought they were drunk. At first it kind of bothered me, not because I thought they were strange, but because they seemed to be able to pray continuously and I was repeating what I said over and over again in the natural because I couldn't think of anything else to say. I guess I was jealous because they had something I didn't.

The more I visited and listened to the pastor, the more I thought about joining, but I kept putting it off. Sometimes in order for me to move, a little fire has to be placed under me and THE LORD KNOWS EXACTLY HOW TO HEAT ME UP! My ex-husband moved to Tennessee to be closer to the children and I brought him to church with us one Sunday. He enjoyed the service so much and decided that he was going to join "my church." How was he going to join "my church" before I joined "my church?" How dare he become a member of "my church" before me?! I was not going to let that happen! I decided that we would take the new members classes together and become members at the same time. You see how THE LORD worked it out. HE IS SO AWESOME!

I was growing spiritually, but I was also struggling financially. One day I was flipping through the channels and came across a Christian network and due to the sermons I heard at church and the sermons I heard on the Christian network, my whole mindset began to change. I remembered this particular network from my childhood. As a child, I didn't want to watch that channel. Whenever the programming started, I would run to the television and turn it off before the host or hostess started talking. It was like a race to the finish line and I would win. As a child, I had to go to church and I decided that if I couldn't do anything to avoid going, I would control whether I listened or not. So, when the preacher would get ready to give his sermon, I would go to sleep. I did this from time to time. There were times when

I decided to listen but I would begin to cry and I didn't know why. Once, my cousin told my aunt that I was crying in church and my aunt told her that it was THE HOLY SPIRIT. I didn't know what she meant.

My pastor and the ministers from the Christian network were teaming up on me with their sermons and I didn't know what to do. I was beginning to see JESUS in a different light and HE was beginning to show me, ME! I would listen the minister's talk about finances and GOD'S LOVE and then go to church and my pastor would talk about forgiveness. The next week they would switch topics on me and it was more than my mind could take. I didn't understand at the time what they meant when they would say,"THE LORD IS JEHOVAH JIRAH (MY PROVIDER)." I couldn't understand it because I was behind on bills and I eventually filed Chapter 13 and 7. I was broke and yes at the time I didn't think it would make a difference if I paid my tithes and offerings. At my home church in Mississippi, paying tithes was not mandatory. We were only required to pay a pastor's fee of $20 dollars and sometimes I didn't pay that. If I wanted to pay my tithes I could have, but it was up to me. If I had a bill to pay and I needed a portion of the tithe to pay the bill, I paid the bill and spent the rest on something else. I thought I was my source. I thought I was responsible for my life, my education and everything else I had. I even went as far as to tell THE LORD that I would take care of the finances and HE could take care of everything else and that is how I ended up filing Chapter 13 and 7 bankruptcy. I took care of the finances all right—not!

My relationship with JESUS really took a turn after the church began to have conferences for women and it was then that I really began to believe that there was more to JESUS than I thought. The women seemed to really love HIM and maybe, just maybe, I didn't know everything about HIM after all. I was broke and broken. I had to pretend to enjoy my job and pretend that my finances were fine because who has ever heard of a broke teacher, especially one who teaches economics?! At the end of every service, several invitations would be given and one of them was to receive the gift of THE HOLY SPIRIT. I wanted that gift so bad. I tried to receive the gift several times because there were only two requirements. First, you had to be saved and second, you had to ask THE LORD for it. I had not received the evidence yet, but my finances were in bad shape and I needed THE LORD TO INTERVENE. I NEEDED TO PRAY TO THE LORD WITHOUT ANY INTERFERENCE! Pastor gave the invitation one Sunday and because of my desperation, I received my gift! All I could do was buck my eyes and cover my lips because I was so amazed. This was something that had never happened to me. I just couldn't believe it! I am thankful THE LORD loved me enough to have a gift for me. HE

REALLY DID LOVE ME! DO YOU KNOW HOW IT FEELS WHEN YOU BELIEVE NO ONE LOVES YOU AND IF THEY SAY THEY DO, IT COMES WITH A PRICE?! JESUS LOVES ME! HE LOVES ME! ME! Chywanda Faye Watson! The one who was abused and thought she was made wrong! The one who thought she was so ugly and disgusting! The one who thought the dirt under her shoes was more important than the person wearing the shoes! The one who had the abortion and tried to commit suicide! The one whose marriage ended in divorce! The one who told GOD that she would take care of the finances and **allow HIM TO TAKE CARE OF EVERYTHING ELSE!** HE LOVES ME!

After receiving THE GIFT OF THE HOLY SPIRIT, Pastor reminded us that we were not created to be "pew warmers." We were supposed to be serving THE LORD in some way, because HE HAS A PLAN AND A PURPOSE FOR US. I decided I wanted to learn more and I wanted to do more. I wanted to know JEHOVAH JIREH. I wanted to trust JESUS and I wanted to take HIM AT HIS WORD. I wanted to believe what HE said. I wanted HIM to be the HEAD OF MY LIFE. I needed to know that I could trust HIM. I had been celibate for about two years and I thought about being in a relationship. I asked THE LORD if I messed up, fornicated, if HE would still love me and HE said YES. I began to weep so heavily because HE loved me so much. I did not mess up and I made the decision that I would not be intimate with a man who was not my husband. This gift that has been reserved and kept by GOD for 17 years will not be opened until he (my husband) finds me. THE LORD said in HIS WORD, *"Whoso findeth a wife, findeth a good thing, and obtaineth favour of the LORD." (Proverbs 18:22)* I believe that because of HIS love for me, I am somebody's good thing and THE LORD IS VERY CLEAR ABOUT WHO IS SUPPOSED TO FIND WHOM. I want my husband to know that I was worth the wait and I want him to know that he was important enough to wait for.

THE LORD had to break some things off of me. HE broke pride, unforgiveness, self-pity, self-righteousness, bitterness, anger, jealously, poverty, lust, and other things off of me. I had to go through deliverance many times. The Deliverance Ministry is awesome and it was important for me to be delivered from everything. I thought I had forgiven my father and my mother, but I still had unforgiveness in my heart. I couldn't serve GOD and receive everything HE has for me, until I dealt with the issues of my heart. If you are trying to get yourself together by yourself, stop! GOD WANTS YOU JUST THE WAY YOU ARE—BROKEN, MISUNDERSTOOD, HURTING, AND ANY WAY YOU COME. HE IS WAITING FOR YOU! If you are ready to give it to JESUS AND BE FREE, then say this prayer out loud:

Heavenly Father, I come to you, recognizing that I am a sinner in need, acknowledging Jesus Christ as my Lord and Savior. I now turn to Jesus and trust Him with my life. I surrender my will to Him. I believe that He was born of a virgin, died on the Cross, and now lives. Thank you Father for forgiving me of all my sins. Come into my heart and make me the person you created me to be. Fill me with Your Holy Spirit. I am now your child. If I died tonight, Heaven would be my home. In Jesus Name, Amen

CHAPTER 7

Scripture: Psalm 32:1-Blessed is he whose transgression is forgiven, whose sin is covered.

The LORD is taking me from glory to glory and I find myself loving HIM more and more each day. He is an awesome FATHER! Because of HIM, I have been able to maintain a good relationship with my father. I can honestly say that I love my father. He made some terrible mistakes when he was younger, but who hasn't? He accepted THE LORD as his SAVIOR and lives a relatively quiet life. He is hard working and he will do whatever he can to help anyone who is having problems with their car even if it is just giving people instructions on how to do the job and that is only because of his age and physical ability. My mother is still beautiful and I love her also. I pray that my story touches the lives of many who may have been abused and misused only to find THE LORD in the end. Without HIS unconditional love, I would be filled with hate and anger. What kind of life is that? HE LOVES ME AND I KNOW IT!

Prom 1986

Senior Portraits

6ᵗʰ grade and pregnant   Age 4

Daddy Lonnie, Me and Momma Bessie

CPSIA information can be obtained
at www.ICGtesting.com
Printed in the USA
BVHW041849011220
594619BV00009B/14